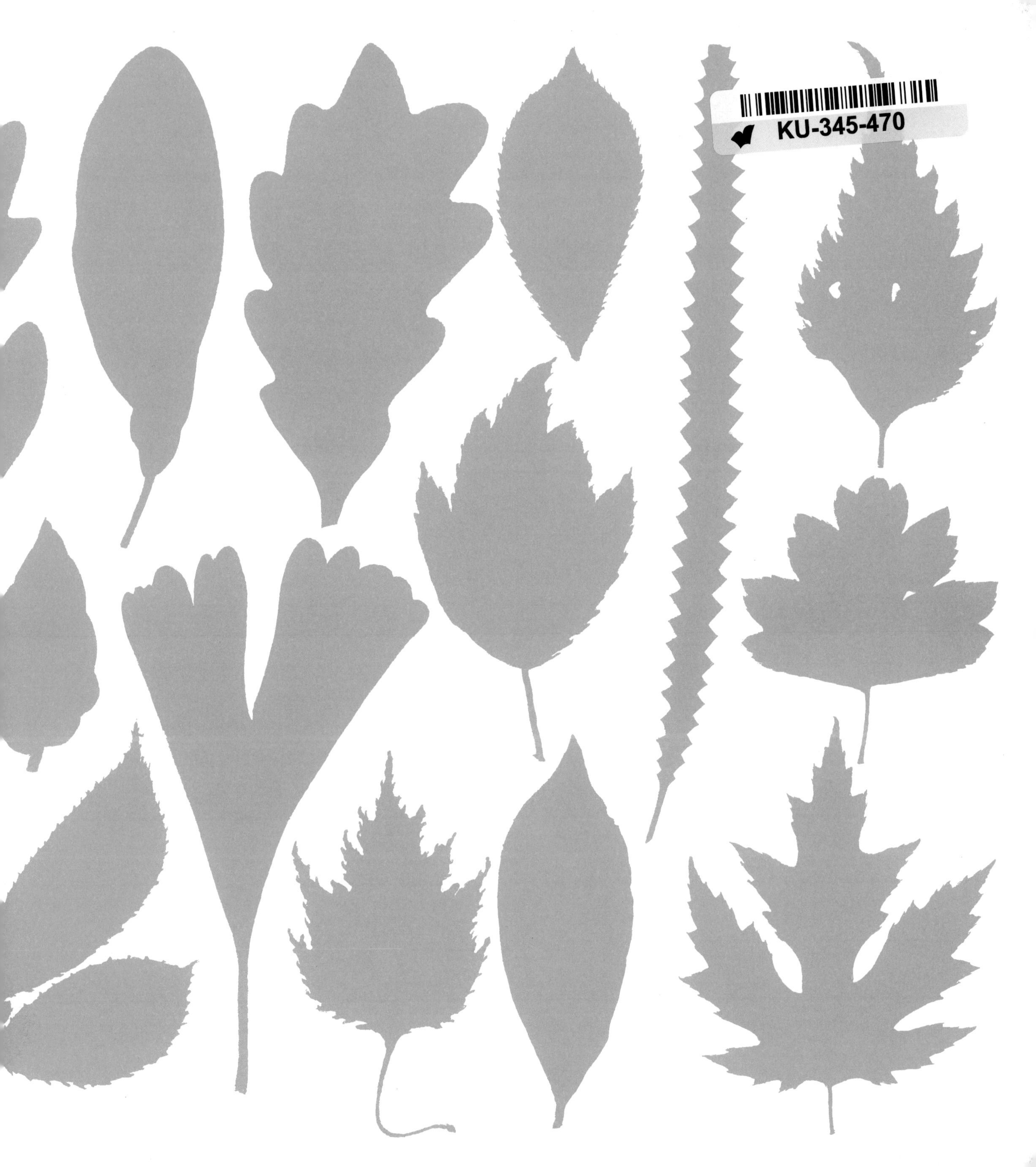

THE WAY WE LIVE
alfresco

STAFFORD CLIFF

THE WAY WE LIVE *alfresco*

WITH OVER 300 COLOUR PHOTOGRAPHS BY

GILLES DE CHABANEIX

THE WAY WE LIVE
alfresco

Half-title Alfresco style above the rooftops of Marrakesh. *Frontispiece* A terrace in Corsica. *Opposite* In a Normandy garden.

INTRODUCTION

Opposite
Although alfresco living is perhaps more usually associated with warm weather and sunny climates, this unusual hideaway in a Quebec garden looks an attractive enough haven in the winter snows.

The French doors to the terrace of a Corsican house are ajar; outside, a table and chairs have been set up with little attention to orderly arrangement. A bottle of wine – open of course – glasses, bread and olives complete the foreground of this beguiling scene. Beyond the terrace the view opens out: a vista of woods and distant hills, all clothed in a light heat haze. Elsewhere, in a verdant Normandy garden, copiously planted with tall trees which create plentiful shade, an as yet unoccupied hammock is slung between two conveniently positioned trunks. Such simple scenes go to the heart of what most people understand by 'alfresco', whose dictionary definition is no more complicated than 'in the open air', which in itself reflects the broader definitions explored by this book.

But the urge to live alfresco is by no means only a product of more relaxed, contemporary lifestyles; pretty well every age and culture have come up with their own interpretation of life outside. Illustrations of the enclosed gardens of Ancient Egypt, for instance, show a formal layout of plant groupings divided by irrigation trenches, pools filled with fish, all for the delectation of the occupants of the seats placed in vine-shaded arbours. The Persian garden, the subject of so many miniatures and graphically represented in carpet designs, was a formal paradise of fruit trees, flower beds and canals, where the privileged strolled, listened to music and enjoyed other entertainments. From such models evolved the Mughal garden, with 'rooms' outside, in which furniture was given as much importance as in the interiors of the palaces to which they were attached; rills and fountains provided the water sounds which complemented peacock calls and the strains of music from the garden pavilions. The influence of Islamic garden design spread across north Africa to southern Spain, where some of the finest examples of the style still exist in Granada. Their external areas (*patios*) are defined by high walls, reflective waterways, majestic pillars and colonnades, to create a more lasting impression than that left by the richly decorated interiors of the surrounding complex of buildings.

Enclosure of open areas around and within the home as an extension of the home is common to cultures around the world. Large walled gardens are mentioned by Homer; the Romans brought the garden into the centre of the house as a vital adjunct to domestic life, surrounding an internal courtyard with a colonnaded atrium or peristyle, a model repeated in countless monasteries and grand houses from central Asia to western Europe. In Japan, the combining of outside and inside living was taken even further in the development of houses which had no conventional walls at all. Semi-transparent panels of rice paper could

be moved aside to reveal secluded private gardens, sometimes only a few feet wide, but designed to symbolize the entire universe. And the concept of rooms open to the outside world remains prevalent throughout the Far East and Indonesia, notably on the island of Bali, where the style has been applied to upmarket hotel and house design, and exported to influence domestic architecture as far away as Los Angeles and Sydney.

In northern Europe, a wider view of the outside world, perhaps framed by a gateway, arch or row of trees, had become part of architectural planning by the fifteenth century. Staircases, terraces, decorative planting and hedges linked garden and house. The spectacular grounds of Versailles, laid out in the seventeenth century, were conceived as a vast outdoor drawing room, intended for the recreation of the huge French court. The people who strolled around the elaborate parterres were as important an element in the whole ensemble as the statuary and fountains; upper rooms looked down on flower beds planted to resemble elaborately patterned carpets. Later, and notably in colonial countries like India, Australia, Canada and South Africa, the veranda came to the fore as a device for extending the activities of inside rooms towards the outside. Here, families could relax in the cool of the evening, business visitors might be welcomed, or estate workers briefed. Those attached to elegant households were often furnished with elaborate pieces in cane, wicker or wrought iron. In the American South, especially, the veranda became an important extra room, its status often emphasized by the addition of soaring white Doric columns and wide two-storey galleries. More modest dwellings across America might make do with a porch area, sufficient for a couple of iron seats or a rocking chair.

Modernist domestic architecture in the United States has seen the development of houses which take substantial account of the surrounding landscape, absorbing nature and blurring the boundaries between inside and outside. Architects such as Philip Johnson and Richard Neutra used walls of glass to create sensations of openness and airiness. Russell Wright famously created a house at Garrison, New York, in a disused quarry, in which boulders and trees figured among the interior furniture and the fireplace was a crevice in the rock wall. This spirit of 'minimum intervention' inspired architects to explore all kinds of ways of extending the space inside the house, using such devices as rooms without conventional walls, roll-up shutters, glass panels which sink into the floor or which can be rolled effortlessly aside. Architectural planting, too, came to be used as a device for relating the outside to the inside; in the purist alfresco house, interior and exterior are parts of the same, continuous experience and virtually interchangeable.

For city dwellers, the alfresco ideal of the past two decades has been associated with access to a second home, a place in the country or, better still, in another country, preferably one with a benevolent climate. Cheaper travel has created more opportunities to enjoy, and eventually to demand, certain aspects of an alfresco lifestyle, in which rustic austerity and simplicity, a closeness to nature, can be reckoned the ultimate extravagance. The kitchen may be replaced by a fire on a beach, electric lighting by candles, and the bathroom by a shower amid palm trees. Lifestyle magazines and books have reflected these new tastes and options: they are photogenic and represent a kind of anti-opulence which has become effectively the new luxury. In countries such as Greece, Turkey, Kenya, Morocco and Indonesia, architects and designers have created sophisticated, entirely contemporary structures, both private and public, in local materials and vernacular styles.

Design-conscious inhabitants of London, New York, Los Angeles, Paris, Berlin or Rome could not remain unaffected by such images of successful alfresco design. In Europe, those fortunate enough to have a roof-terrace or balcony furnished them as extra rooms. Those with porches and verandas in America or Australia made them into real extensions of their houses. It became usual for cafés and bars in temperate climates to offer terrace seating – often with outdoor heating – even in the winter months. The garden or the backyard became the ultimate room, to be the subject of endless television makeover programmes and completed by wooden decking, pebbles, gravel, slate shards, bark chips and, of course, a dining table and chairs.

Gastronomy, indeed, never seems very far from the social side of alfresco living. A number of the images in the final chapter of the book bring to the fore the pleasures of consuming simple, delicious food and drink outside. Feasts, markets, open-air restaurants and, inevitably, picnics reflect the broadest possible interpretation of living alfresco, yet are at its very heart. The Japanese eat outside as a celebratory aesthetic experience; the Chinese honour their dead in graveside feasts; in the West, the picnic was a recognized accompaniment to the medieval hunt and later became an important literary and artistic metaphor for the good life in the nineteenth century, when the evocation of the rustic idyll, typified by Monet's *Déjeuner sur l'herbe* of 1865, began a process which has continued and intensified ever since: living happily between within and without. So, if all other alfresco options fail, then just pack a hamper, assemble a few friends, and head for your local park, the beach, or the open countryside.

Preceding pages
Eating outside is surely one of the most important aspects of an alfresco lifestyle. Pleasant outside dining areas can always be created by simple arrangements of furniture in an engagingly informal setting. Here, the placing of garden chairs and a sturdy wooden table – presumably within easy reach of the kitchen door – has formed an effective eating space without the construction of formal veranda, terrace or patio. Other essential elements in the success of this enticing Provençal scene are the shade offered by the overhanging branches of the tree and the rudimentary cover which connects it to the wall of the house.

Colonizing and formalizing the space around the home lie at the heart of the great garden traditions. From the courtyards of Islamic architecture to the confections of seventeenth-century France, or even contemporary roof-terraces, the well-appointed garden has always been an essential extension of living areas, a place for strolling, reflection and conversation. Orderly planting, ornament and statuary define such spaces for our enjoyment; the formal interior thus has its outside equivalent. This representation (*left*) of a classical French garden, complete with a central axis aligned with the principal portico of the associated façade, is in fact a painted wall panel in Louhisaari, a Finnish country house renowned for its decoration in the French style.

This modern interpretation of the formal garden with central axis is an entirely appropriate complement to a traditional house on the island of Ibiza (*right*). The rectilinear parterres exactly reflect the form of the whitewashed house, effectively a series of cubes, each one of which represents a room giving on to a single common space. Although this garden has a paved strip as its central element rather than a rill or short canal and a large water bowl instead of a fountain, there is nevertheless a Moorish feel about the whole ensemble, a vestigial recollection of a past occupation.

The rich, dark colours of the local soil have inspired this sculptural composition around the pool of a private Los Angeles house (*right*). Solid masonry blocks of various sizes create a constantly changing play of light and shade; their brownish hues reflect a deliberate drawing of inspiration from nature, a theme continued inside the house. Around the pool itself irregularly shaped slabs of rock reaffirm the design's debt to natural forms.

CHAPTER 1

OUTSIDE THE HOME

Reclaiming Nature

Simply stepping outside the enclosed interiors of the home – house or apartment – constitutes a first stage in the alfresco lifestyle. The traditional house in whatever form or culture usually has a garden or outdoor space attached to it; the colonizing and formalizing of that area is often the main way of creating a relationship between inside and outside. Certainly applicable to the great garden styles (Moorish, Italian, French and English), the principle can hold equally good for a porch, a rooftop, a deck, a balcony on which pots of plants have been grouped to formal effect.

Yet, as many of the photographs on the following pages amply demonstrate, the initiation into the alfresco lifestyle can be engagingly simple and informal. Sometimes it is sufficient to set a bench down in a meadow or parkland; sometimes a simple chair parked in the shade of a tree will create a tranquil corner for the enjoyment of the outside world. Or the point of focus may be a swimming-pool or water feature, especially in warm and benevolent climates, sited to take advantage of the natural scenery around. Even pathways and boardwalks in exciting and original forms open up the landscape or lead us across lakeshore or seashore.

The most beguiling images in this chapter, though, must surely be those of shaded, often slightly unkempt gardens, in which a table and a few chairs or benches have been distributed beneath a tree, presumably in anticipation of an alfresco lunch and consequent convivial conversation. And in a somewhat more ordered environment, similar scenes may be repeated beneath an awning or pergola, or on a deck or terrace, evolving all the year round.

Preceding pages
A bench with a view: the simplest and most immediate way of starting to reclaim the natural world surrounding any habitation is to place some rudimentary article of furniture in it. In this case, the oddly reassuring form of the traditional slatted bench looks out from a Provençal garden towards cultivated fields and vineyards beyond.

In public park or in private garden or, indeed, in a village street, the placing of benches or chairs marks a first step in alfresco living, in the reclamation and ordering of the natural world. Such arrangements are inevitably the focus for conversation pieces, as in this leisurely scene in a Barcelona park (*left above*). Harder to fathom is the reason for this row of ill-matched chairs and their attendant occupants in an Umbrian village (*left below*): waiting for a shop or stall to open, perhaps?

A garden bench surrounded by a profusion of foliage is sufficient to create a small area of repose and contemplation in a Provençal garden (*right above*). These qualities are given a public face by the occupants of a more clearly utilitarian structure in a Paris park (*right below*).

This stretch of parkland (*above*) lies just beyond the more strictly formal planting of a Mauritian garden: an ideal spot to pause and enjoy the natural splendours of the island.

The unexpected location amid olive trees and the unorthodox shape of this pool provide an intriguing spectacle for whoever decides to occupy this invitingly placed seat in a Nice garden (*above*).

Any spot in a well-tended garden – either amid the formal Roman Renaissance terraces of the Villa d'Este at Tivoli (*left*) or on the more informal grass of a Scottish park (*opposite*) – can be transformed into an informal but elegant conversation area. In both cases dramatic effect is derived from the juxtaposition of extravagant foliage with the graceful formality of the painted wooden furniture whose light colour makes it a focal point in the overall design.

For many people, such scenes as these must represent the purest essence of alfresco living: rays of sunlight falling through the branches of trees on to a carefully chosen spot for a meal outside. A fresh island light illuminates parts of this sheltered garden of a house on the Île de Ré, off the west coast of France (*left above*). The stronger light and heat of the region in summer is effectively filtered by the foliage overhanging an enticing table setting in a Provence garden (*left below*). Light furniture can be moved easily and folded for storage at the end of the day.

These two gardens also benefit from the combination of the play of light and shade provided by trees and shrubs, but in very different climates and with very different qualities of light. Wooden 'Adirondack-style' chairs provide the elements for alfresco relaxation in a Provence garden (*right above*). A more eclectic mix of seating provides the owners of this Irish country house with the chance to enjoy the much-appreciated fine days of summer (*right below*). Since there is no formal seating area, the chairs can be moved to follow the sun.

Sometimes it is the world beyond, the larger landscape or indeed an expanse of sky or the setting sun, which provide the visually dramatic elements in alfresco living. A swimming-pool is often the focus of outside activity during the summer months – certainly, in such benevolent climates as that of Tuscany (*right*). In this case, the view from the poolside includes a fair swathe of classic Tuscan countryside: hills punctuated by the tall fingers of cypress trees and completed by a medieval defensive tower. The pool itself may also be an important outside feature, as in this Nice garden (*overleaf*), where the unusual shape makes a striking addition to the surrounding planting of olive trees and ornamental shrubs.

A central theme of the Islamic garden is water, whether as pond, pool, basin, rill or canal. It is the focal point of the enclosed garden, symbol of paradise, and as much part of a dwelling as the rooms within. The surrounds of this pool in Hammamet, Tunisia, evoke the antiquity of the country's culture (*left above*). In Granada, Spain, the gardens of the Generalife (*left below*), are among the greatest achievements of Moorish Spain, supreme refinements of outside living: a formal water feature, box hedges, terracotta pots – quintessential Mediterranean.

The traditional domestic architecture of Bali – much imitated throughout south-east Asia and the Pacific – has an openness which makes distinctions between living inside and living outside almost meaningless (*right above*). 'Houses' may consist of pavilion-like structures which give on to a communal court, often embellished with a water feature. Pools and fountains have a peculiarly soothing quality in warm climates; for instance, it would be hard to imagine a more tranquil spot than this ornamental stretch of water in a Mauritian garden (*right below*).

To act as a real focal point of alfresco living a pool should ideally be surrounded by an area sufficient to allow all the associated activities of sunbathing, eating and drinking, or simply hanging out. This very private area attached to a house in Saint-Rémy-de-Provence (*above*) has all those qualities, with the additional attraction of formal planting; the simple rectangle of the pool echoes the large opening into the house.

The owners of this villa in Puglia, Italy, decided to take the larger view in the siting of this pool (*above*). Effectively, the whole of the surrounding landscape forms a varied and varying backdrop to whatever activities take place on the extensive paved area in the foreground. The powerful effect of the whole ensemble derives from the large scale of each of its components.

Preceding pages
Two very contrasting 'takes' on the alfresco environment – one closed, one open, yet both are peculiarly expressive of their individual climates and environments. A garden in Marrakesh (originally established by Louis Majorelle) is defined by a sense of enclosure (albeit with openwork *treillage*) to create a demi-paradise of luxuriant planting and formal water features. In strict contrast is this Belgian garden and pool, formal in its own way and still presenting a dramatic vista under the low winter sun.

The interaction of home and habitation with living outside can be the inspiration for some fascinating architectural incursions, in sympathetic materials, into the landscape or waterscape (*these pages* and *overleaf*). The descent to sea bathing from a villa on the French Riviera is achieved by a complex system of pathways, a bridge to the rocky foreshore and final steps to the water (*above*).

The Atacama desert in central Chile is one of the driest areas in the world and possessed of a dramatic landscape. One hotel there hit on the intriguing idea of building pathways (*above*) out into the land around it, complete with resting places, so that guests could more easily enjoy the immediate countryside around. The result has something of an art installation about it.

The enticing effect of walkways: they lead the eye to anticipate and the feet to explore – an overwater cabin in Tahiti (*above left*); a guest cottage on a Chilean estate (*above right*); a chance to fish at Chiloë, Chile (*opposite left*); or walk out above the treetops in Rangoon (*opposite right*).

Sometimes the most relaxing and satisfying moments of alfresco living are created by the simple, happy coincidence of engaging vistas and casually placed chairs. At opposite ends of France – in Brittany (*left*) and in Provence (*opposite*) – twin *transatlantiques* look out over magnificent vistas, from areas close to houses transformed into impromptu viewing points.

Appropriate materials and careful planting combine to define that area close to the house which is the ideal terrain for living, eating and conversing outside. Wooden decking, especially, is ideal for delineating such spaces – here, in San Francisco (*opposite*) and in Brittany (*right*) – and looks utterly at home with the surrounding shrubbery and garden furniture. It also provides a good base for an outsize pebble or a plant.

Not only is this alfresco dining arrangement sited among shrubs and trees in a Moroccan garden (*left*), its very *faux-bois* form (although executed in solid masonry) reflects the vegetation which surrounds it – yet another novel way of reclaiming nature that first came into fashion in the late nineteenth century.

The use of natural forms and materials to create outdoor furniture seems to strike a common chord throughout the world. Seating in the form of toadstools embellishes this imaginative set-piece in a Manila garden (*right above*). Hefty cross-sections of timber have been used to create matching benches and tables in the courtyard of a house in Kenya. (*right below*).

A graceful awning supported by simple wooden poles has been sufficient to create this oddly formal alfresco dining area in a Provence garden (*opposite*). Nevertheless, there is a sense of rightness about the whole arrangement, just as there is about the placing of the table and chairs beneath a wisteria-hung pergola in a magnificent Umbrian garden (*right*).

CHAPTER 2

TRANSITIONAL SPACES

Verandas, Terraces, Patios, Conservatories

Halfway between private and public worlds are those parts of the home which give immediate access to the street, garden or parkland. Most of such areas illustrated here can accommodate all the normal daily activities of domestic life – eating, drinking and conversation – while providing room for container planting and the display of interesting objects. These are the places which open up the home to the outside world and, as such, are central to the whole concept of alfresco.

Their form, of course, varies according to climate, topography and local traditions. In sunny, sub-tropical regions, there is an obvious concern to provide shade and protection from the effects of heat and, conceivably, from heavy rain. Of particular interest are the traditional houses of Japan, Thailand and Bali; overhanging eaves and movable screen-walls create areas in which the interior moves seamlessly into the exterior and in which much of the social life of the group or family takes place. In Western environments, the loggia, balcony and terrace provide opportunities for extending the house into the open air. Enclosed courtyards and secluded town gardens feature here; the old houses of Morocco, notably, often have internal courts which serve as communal spaces in themselves but also bring light and air into lower-storey rooms.

Many of the structures illustrated here are enlivened by planting and the arrangement of furniture and ornament: humble front-door porches to grand colonnaded verandas, loggias, courtyards and even big-city pocket parks. The variety is considerable but they are all revealing examples of the search for a pleasing conjunction between interior confinement and exterior freedom.

One of the first and most important spaces in the transition from home to the world outside is the front porch, a place where visitors may be welcomed or, in the case of this highly decorated, neoclassical example in Stockholm (*left*), a spot for a brief pause before entering the house. Similarly, the transition from one part of a formal walled garden – here, in Sri Lanka (*opposite*) – may be marked by some form of seating from which the distant vista can be contemplated and passers-by engaged in conversation in the cooler evening air.

If the weather and climate are suitably benevolent, there is a very natural inclination, common to many cultures, to turn the area immediately around the house into a space for leisurely relaxation and contemplation. In these examples from Hampi, Karnataka, India (*above*), Cuba (*opposite left*)and Normandy (*opposite right*), the extended porch and backyard/patio have become additional 'rooms' to the main dwelling.

Overleaf
Even in snow-bound Quebec, the advantages of verandas and balconies are evident. They provide viewing points, a means of communication between various points of the house, for children's play and opportunities for decorative extravagance. In summer, of course, they can act as real extensions of the life of the home – a place for eating, drinking and conversation.

3854

Overhanging decorative features protect the structure of the traditional Thai house (*left*). They also create verandas and extended porches which symbolize the transition from natural setting to artificial structure and add status to the front door. They also provide an important forum for family life.

Although as ornate in a very different style as the Bangkok porch (*opposite*), this splendid Victorian entrance to a Quebec house (*right*) is less a place for meeting and conversation than an announcement of the importance of the house and its owners. Yet, the extensions on either side of the two pillars suggest that the architect was conscious of a need to make a gradual transition from the street to the indoors.

Halfway between private and public worlds, verandas, terraces and, eventually, gardens provide us with places of pause between interior lives and the larger human activity beyond. Such areas may be simple and humble in structure and furnishing (here, in south-west France)(*above*) or elaborate in architecture and decoration (*opposite*) to become truly a room outside. This extension to a Tunisian villa, for instance, is furnished with ceramics and stoneware in a manner which clearly suggests that it is intended as a formal addition to the rooms within, as well as a friendly welcome to visitors.

Verandas and loggias can serve many and varied purposes. They can clearly act as extra dining areas; this particularly sumptuous example (*above*) is attached to a house on the island of Mauritius. Apart from acting as alfresco dining rooms, such adjuncts to this Mexican dwelling are ideal places for simply sitting; they are useful, too, as settings for larger objects, such as free-standing sculpture or earthenware pots, whose material and size make them less suitable for interior display (*opposite*).

Such climates as that of the Mediterranean which have the good fortune to enjoy fine weather for a substantial part of the year can afford a particularly relaxed approach to alfresco living. A loosely defined patio or backyard (*above*), a chair or two, and perhaps a canopy – like this combination adjoining a house in Salina on Lipari, in the Aeolian Islands – are sufficient to permit the savouring of the combined delights of shelter from the heat and a profusion of foliage.

In very warm climates, such as that enjoyed by Tahiti, there is a lot to be said for paying extra careful attention to the appropriateness of the materials used both for the construction of open areas and for the furniture (*above*). Formal indoor chairs would look out of place here; more successful effects can be achieved with cane, twig and articles of durable local craftsmanship.

As halfway, transitional spaces between interior and exterior, loggias, verandas, terraces and patios provide ideal settings for eating and drinking alfresco, with the possibility of conversation and relaxed reflection thrown in for good measure. In warm climates, or during the summer months in more temperate zones, such areas can easily serve as additional 'outside rooms', accommodating tables and chairs to create extra dining space. A few items of traditional rustic furniture and a paved area adjoining the house, like this example (*left*), on the Île de Ré, off the west coast of France, can be combined to create a robust and flexible place for leisurely consumption and contemplation.

More formal in construction and arrangement than the preceding French example is this sitting area in a splendid tiled loggia adjoining a house on Mauritius (*right*). Although the materials and forms are entirely appropriate to what is, effectively, a room with only one wall, the whole effect is one of restrained formality. There is very little suggestion of the impromptu here – more a feeling that this area is in fairly constant use and really does constitute an extra room. Tropical plants in wooden planters complete a scene of order and comfort.

Another area of the loggia of the Mauritian house (*p. 67*) is also furnished quite formally, but again the materials are entirely fitting – plantation chairs in native hardwood (*above left*). All the arrangements illustrated on these pages address the outside world with a degree of formality, even the dining area of a traditional Balinese house (*above right*). And Florian, the celebrated café on the great Piazza of St Mark's, Venice, the finest drawing room in Europe, according to Napoleon, has traditionally brought an almost ritualistic feel to the drinking of coffee outside (*opposite*).

58
TEA-ROOM

Bringing the surrounding landscape in: a simple yet robust veranda of a house on Mauritius (*above*) shows how the activities of home – in this case, an elegant bench for conversation – can co-exist and contrast with adjacent farmland.

A veranda such as this other Mauritian example (*above*) can also present myriad possibilities for decorative elaboration. The surrounding rail is delicately intricate, while the hammock – surely one of the essential accoutrements of true alfresco living – is embellished with hanging tassles.

Without the longer view to the surrounding landscape, the veranda or terrace becomes even more a place of transition – part of the house, but also part of the garden, enlivened here by the presence of a caged bird. In this example in Santiago de Chile (*left*), the plants on the terrace seem to continue seamlessly from the planting in the surrounding garden. Still close to the surrounding trees of the garden, yet with some sense of separateness, is this veranda of a house in Rangoon (*opposite*).

A loggia on the grand scale, like this Italianate example (*above*), is a space for ostentatious display and decoration; and, like a cloister, it is a place to stroll and meditate. Ornate statuary and wall-painting complete a scene of opulence and spaciousness.

In a more modern vein, this wide and accommodating loggia (*above*) runs along the garden façade of a magnificent private house on Mauritius. It is clearly substantial enough to provide space for virtually any domestic activity, with the added advantage of a view to the garden beyond the columns. Part of a fine house, yet at the same time an extension of the garden, whose vegetation protrudes over the dividing balustrade; this is a true transitional space between two worlds.

The width of this veranda running along the side of a noble Chilean estate house (*left above*) makes it an ideal spot for family reunions. It can also serve as a place for business – meeting the estate managers and workers, perhaps. In a traditional Thai house in Bangkok (*left below*) the substantial overhanging eaves protect the structure from monsoon rains and create a transitional veranda space between the artifice of the main building and the natural setting which surrounds it. Exterior walls are frequently in the form of moveable screens, so that the lives of the occupants can be enriched by contemplation of the changing seasons and respect for the natural forces immediately beyond the veranda rail.

There is a certain grandeur about both these terrace-verandas, a sense of holding nature at bay, perhaps because of their series of elegant formal columns, which make these spaces effective galleries for viewing the beauties of the gardens beyond and for family living, especially in this example from Mauritius (*right above*). The seating in the grand gallery of a Mallorcan house (*right below*) suggests that it is principally a viewing point for the vistas beyond the building.

The gallery-veranda of this Chilean estate house (*above*) provides sufficient shelter and extra wall-space for a significant extension of the collection of furniture, objects and paintings in the main rooms within.

Part of a private home in Marseilles, this tiled gallery (*above*) is clearly integral to the life of the occupants, for eating and conversation, and with access to several interior rooms. It is wide enough, too, to provide protection from any extremes of weather.

Overleaf
This veranda of a Chilean house serves as an additional room or gallery in which quite formal furniture and decoration look perfectly at home. Its transitional quality, however, is emphasized by the profusion of outside foliage intruding between the columns.

Elegant curves, subtle colours, a tiled frieze and marble floor lend distinction to a courtyard balcony in Havana (*above*).

The overhanging eaves of the veranda of a Shanghai house (*above*) provide the opportunity for decorative embellishment with traditional Chinese fretwork and screens.

Caribbean style: the decorative impulses of the builders of the Bahamas are given full rein in the elaborate woodwork of a series of upper-storey verandas or galleries (*above*).

Another example from the Bahamas (*above*); here, the woodwork is less fanciful and the formal garden and the ocean beyond provides the visual interest for the occupants.

Columns and arches lend dignity to a variety of loggias and verandas; in these examples, the variety of styles of architecture, the use of materials and the glimpses of surrounding planting and architecture establish them as truly integrated spaces that bridge interior and exterior: Saigon (*far left above*); Goa (*left above*); Cuba (*far left below*); Chile (*left below*); Saigon, Florence, Finland (*opposite above, left to right*); Brittany, Guatemala, Istanbul (*opposite below, left to right*).

Viewed from the surrounding garden, which sweeps grandly down to the Hudson river, the colonnade of the veranda of an already magnificent house adds yet another note of formal grandeur (*above*). Much of the summer life of this house takes place here; the furniture is arranged in a number of 'conversation groups', much as it would be in a grand *salon*.

On the same veranda (*above*), metal chairs from the nineteen-forties are mixed with contemporary folding chairs and a bench after a design by Lutyens.

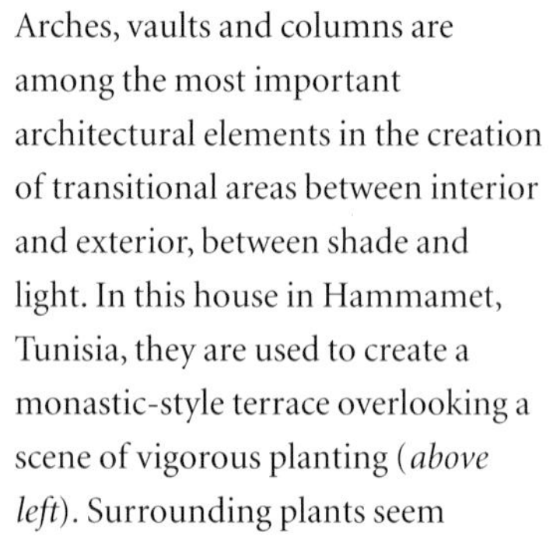

Arches, vaults and columns are among the most important architectural elements in the creation of transitional areas between interior and exterior, between shade and light. In this house in Hammamet, Tunisia, they are used to create a monastic-style terrace overlooking a scene of vigorous planting (*above left*). Surrounding plants seem almost about to take over this shaded dining area of a Guatemalan house (*above right*). The immense height of the ground-floor columns gives an air of sober dignity to the extended porch of this hotel in the Landes area of western France, the property of a renowned French chef, and former hunting lodge (*opposite*).

The town-house balcony, often embellished with decorative cast-iron rails in its nineteenth-century form, provides further welcome access to the outside in urban environments where land is at a premium. Situated above the dust and din of the street in warm climates, it acts as an extension to the upper rooms and, if sheltered by overhanging eaves, an additional place for relaxation. This example, on the street façade of a house in Buenos Aires (*left*), combines the simplest of balcony forms with the most elaborate of guard-rails.

This Athens house (*right above*) enjoys a simple balcony with a straightforward, probably locally made, rail. Much more elaborate was the use of cast-iron for the balconies and verandas of the great nineteenth-century Australian cities. The climate encouraged the development of the veranda and roofed balcony with its accompaniment of intricate cast-iron work, often reminiscent of its use on London town houses, as in these two examples on a Sydney street (*right below*). Much of the cast-iron used throughout the world was prefabricated and bought from (mainly British) manufacturers' catalogues. It has been suggested that the material was used as ships' ballast during its transit, although this seems unlikely, given its relative fragility.

The small roof-terrace or balcony has a universal appeal: most effectively, it offers a private vantage point from which to partake of the visual pleasures of the surrounding garden or the street below. All the examples on these pages have a delightfully secluded air, yet still manage to enjoy the feeling of being in touch with the world at large: Egypt (*opposite*); Naples (*right above*); Mauritius (*far right above*); Marseilles (*right below*); Cévennes (*far right below*).

Open to the garden but well sheltered, this loggia of a Guatemalan house (*opposite*) provides plenty of space for furniture and ornament, making it a real transition from the dark interior of the house to the delights of the vigorous plant life outside. Although many verandas or terraces, often of simple design or construction, are inappropriate for opulent furnishing, this space is so obviously part of the living rooms of the house that the heavier furniture and ornament seem completely at home.

The veranda of this house overlooking the river Nile in Cairo (*right*) shows just what flexibility such an adjunct can have as an extension to the home. Wall decoration, ornament and obviously comfortable furniture declare this a place for recreational conversation, protected from the strong light of day. It also enjoys the advantage of having immediate access to any slight breeze.

Preceding pages
The luxury end of alfresco living: these four terraces are all of very deliberate construction, designed to be part of the house, as well as enjoying outstanding views. Great care has obviously been taken in the choice of furniture, which is in all cases stylish but appropriate to its outdoor function – in Sicily (*p. 96, above* and *below*), Umbria (*p. 97, above*) and in Istanbul (*p. 97, below*).

Less formal than the purpose-built terraces of the preceding examples, but equally attractive and useful in its own way, is the variously named patio or backyard. In both of the cases illustrated here – in Corsica (*left*) and on the Île de Ré, western France (*opposite*) – it has only been necessary to introduce chairs and a table to an area within easy reach of the house to create a wealth of day-long possibilities.

This arrangement of table and chairs outside a home in Guatemala (*above*) seems to have happened at very short notice, with furniture simply shifted from indoors. Note, though, how effective is the subtle green of the shutters and door as a colour for a garden façade.

Trained vegetation to provide shade from direct sunlight in warm climates is often a desirable feature of the backyard. This shaded deck abuts a traditional wooden Thai house in Bangkok (*above*).

Enclosed courtyards offer a rather different alfresco experience to the verandas and terraces of the preceding pages. Without views of the surrounding garden or landscape, they become much more the 'room outside'. Indeed, like the example in Bali (*above*), the interior of the house may open directly on to a walled or fenced space, made more interesting here by a water feature.

There is an almost conservatory feel about this leafy courtyard of a house on the island of Madeira (*above*). Its role as a transitional space is emphasized by the pebbled paving – natural materials put to practical use. The planting is simple but stylish.

Alfresco on a grander scale: two arrangements for family feasts in Rajasthan, India, await the arrival of the participants (*left above* and *below*). In Venice, the fashionable cafés of the great Piazza of St Mark's set out their chairs and tables in symmetrical rows (*opposite*), for once free of people and pigeons.

In urban settings the enclosed small space, private or public, must offer the principal solution to the problem of finding somewhere to indulge our need for a degree of outside living. There is, indeed, a very private air about this paved garden (*above left*) in London adjoining the house of an architect renowned for his minimalist approach to design. A similar feeling of secluded space emanates from a courtyard area planted with small trees in a traditional Marrakesh house (*above right*). And for a moment of pause and contemplation amid the din and bustle of New York, there is always the solution of the 'pocket park', frequently shoe-horned into any suitable gap between the soaring walls of skyscrapers (*opposite*).

This courtyard of a traditional Thai house (*left*) is clearly a seamless extension of the interior, reflecting a culture where contemplation of the natural world is of paramount importance. It also makes an ideal setting for the display of sculpture and ornamental plants.

A similar effect to the interaction of inside and outside, so notable in the Thai house, is achieved in this Normandy home (*right*) by the simple device of glazed sliding doors. The sense of an inner, private courtyard is confirmed by the high retaining fence which further extends the unifying use of wood in the whole ensemble.

The old town of Essaouira, on Morocco's Atlantic coast, is a place of fine houses. This example (*left*), recently restored, is a structure of interlocking terraces and rooms in which the relative absence of conventional doors and windows contributes to a sensation of movement of light and air from *salon* to balcony and to a paved rooftop garden (*pp. 124–125*).

Another traditional Moroccan house – this one in Marrakesh – is centred on an open area (*opposite*) which reinterprets the time-honoured Islamic court in an entirely contemporary way. Finely worked antique wooden doors, however, hint at the seventeenth-century origins of the house, while the floor tiles pick up the patterns of Berber weaving. The whole space is further defined by four orange trees around a low bubble fountain, with four large lanterns and canvas 'Butterfly' chairs.

These two backyards, respectively in Paris (*left above*) and on the Île de Ré (*left below*), have been dramatically enlivened by the presence of climbing plants. And what would otherwise have been relatively drab and anonymous spaces have become vibrant and exciting – a perfect setting for the excursion from the back door to the world outside.

Both of these gardens incorporate in their very design, structure and materials the feeling of outside living. There is a refined rusticity in the use of rough stone for walls and seating in a Mallorcan garden (*right above*). Wood is a dominant theme in the Stockholm garden of a sculptor, where carefully arranged stacks of cut branches provide striking points of focus (*right below*), almost as if the outsize sculpted bird had been gathering materials for its nest.

Simple, hand-painted wall design and a fountain give this Seville courtyard plenty of intricate interest in both aural and visual terms, a legacy perhaps of the Moorish era (*above*).

The high walls of this Moroccan garden (*above*) do offer the prospect of a world beyond their confines in the form of the aperture above the gate, a reminder of larger perspectives; the split bamboo furniture has no doubt been acquired in local markets.

The use of high, unadorned walls is one way of producing a sense of secretiveness, of intimacy, as in this Moroccan garden (*left*), with year-round seating in the form of a built-in rectangular bench. In his Barcelona Pavilion of 1929 – arguably one of the most beautiful modern buildings ever constructed – Mies van der Rohe resorted to the use of high walls to create and define a sequence of beautifully related spaces around a pool let into a wide pedestal of Roman travertine (*opposite*), brilliantly updating Moorish tradition.

Extensions upwards and backwards are one solution for apartment dwellers in large cities, especially one like London (*above*), where 'flats' are often not purpose-built, but part of whole-house conversions.

This back-terrace extension to a London apartment (*above*) has been transformed into a secluded floral haven with the simplest of materials and well-chosen seasonal plants to provide plenty of life.

Colour is provided mainly by the building materials and pots on this delightful sunlit terrace of a Paris house (*above*).

Somewhere between terrace and veranda, these two structures demonstrate confident use of space and cover for larger areas – effectively creating rooftop gardens. Both benefit from luxuriant and profuse planting – the one (*left above*) deep in the Chilean countryside, the other (*left below*) near Rome.

This roof-terrace (*right above*) in the intensely built-up area of central Paris relies for its effectiveness as a space for alfresco eating and relaxation on the presence of as much planting as can reasonably be accommodated in such a small area. In contrast, this delightfully cool-looking terrace of a house in Hammamet, Tunisia, can simply enjoy the view of the rich vegetation beyond (*right below*). Both schemes, however, make extensive use of white as a positive colour.

The breathing spaces of large cities: a private roof-terrace in New York has the luxury of enjoying the magnificent skyline of the city at night (*above*). In downtown San Francisco virtually every flat area visible here among the high-rise buildings has been converted into a pocket park or terrace (*opposite*) for office-workers.

Overleaf
This restored house in Essaouira, Morocco, is topped by a terrace that is, in effect, an additional, roofless sitting room, open to the town at large but also intensely private. There is very little clutter here, yet the simplest of materials and structures manages to convey an air of comfort; these include parasols fixed to the walls on pivoting arms, recessed wall lights and plenty of opportunities for just lounging.

C H A P T E R 3

ROOMS OUTSIDE

Gazebos, Belvederes, Pavilions, Summerhouses

There is a perennial, child-like fascination with the idea of a 'little house', the hideaway at the bottom of the garden where we experience a sense of release from the orderly demands of life at home. An interesting variation on the theme of separateness from some main, formal centre has begun to show itself in modern hotel design, especially in tropical and sub-tropical regions. A number of examples occur on the following pages of structures which house hotel guests separately from the main hub or service complex. Some can be complete mini-residences; others may be stylish alfresco dining areas; most importantly, they convey a feeling of privacy and a sense of being at home. Most of them have been designed or constructed in ways which are sensitive to indigenous tradition and the local landscape.

The Western 'take' on the 'little house' concept is represented by summerhouses and pavilions of various styles. There is always a feeling about such places that they should be used for some strenuously creative purpose – writing or musical composition – or for activities entirely clandestine.

Once again, the influence of south-east Asian architecture , especially that of Bali, is abundantly apparent in a number of the structures illustrated here, characterized by wide overhanging roofs supported on pillars. The 'walls' are generally open, permitting views of garden, vegetation, or the wider landscape beyond, making possible a style of living in which interior and exterior are of equal importance.

Simple, timeless, yet sophisticated, this pool-side shelter at a Kenyan resort (*above*) typifies modern developments in hotel design in tropical regions. This inside/outside structure uses local and immediately available materials to create a space which reflects and respects indigenous styles and cultures.

This shelter in a Balinese garden (*above*) uses local materials so effectively as to appear to be almost part of the surrounding undergrowth.

Typical of a new generation of 'decentralized' hotels, this Bangkok establishment has a number of open areas, sheltered by wooden structures in traditional Thai styles (*above*) that permit guests to relax away from the main reception and service complex. The temple-like roof adds status to the structure.

This alfresco dining area in a Mauritian garden (*above*) uses rustic materials and construction to create an alternative environment to the formalities of the main house. Lightweight bentwood chairs complete an ensemble which is straightforward yet utterly effective.

The design of this elegant lakeside pavilion in Sweden has clearly been inspired by the early nineteenth-century European vogue for chinoiserie (*above*); it looks like the ideal place to write a novel, compose a symphony, or conduct a liaison.

The spatial possibilities of a sturdy cottage in a Scottish fishing village have been substantially enhanced by the addition of a conservatory of Victorian inspiration (*above*).

This tented pavilion in a nature camp and wilderness hideaway on the Indonesian island of Moyo (*above*) is a fine example of new trends in luxury lodging, whereby local, natural materials are used to create environments very much at one with the surrounding land – movable luxury indeed!

Native Balinese architecture, like this pavilion (*above*), is notable for its qualities of openness, reflecting a culture in which the appreciation of the beauties of the island's flora plays a central role; a massively overhanging roof provides protection from the rains, while allowing the free circulation of air in the often humid conditions.

A number of low-impact hotels are available to visitors at Uluru, formerly known as Ayers Rock, in Australia's Red Centre (*right above* and *below*). This luxury tented resort makes a sympathetic modern contrast to the natural drama of the surrounding landscape.

Garden paths sometimes get forgotten as design features, because of their utilitarian aspect as a means of getting from one place to another. Yet, they can easily be as important as buildings or planting in our efforts to control and manage an outside environment. The large-pebble pathways in this cactus garden in Baja California (*opposite*), for instance, are a sculptural presence amid the sparse planting, as they lead to the tented hammock in the centre.

The need for a room outside, a hideaway from the main residence and its demands, resonates through many cultures. Such buildings may have a specific purpose – a music room or a writer's retreat – or may simply be places apart, for reflection, rest and contemplation as, one suspects, are these two structures: the one in a Swedish park (*left*), the other in a Balinese palace garden (*opposite*).

An essential feature of the public-park movement of the nineteenth century was the bandstand. This particular snow-laden example (*above*) is in Quebec.

Openwork Chinese trellis gives a lightness and transparency of feel to this traditional pavilion (*above*) in Shanghai.

This little summer pavilion (*above*) in a Stockholm garden makes an ideal place for quiet study and contemplation.

Eliel Saarinen designed this summerhouse (*above*) for his garden at Hvittsträsk, Finland, in the first decade of the twentieth century – a distinguished design reflecting the architect's Art and Crafts roots.

A simple summerhouse in a Stockholm garden (*above*) provides a light and airy place for relaxation. In this case, it is a welcome alternative to a very busy household that also includes the sculptor owner's studio.

In the Chilean rain-forest is the estate of a prominent American billionaire who is also a conservationist on a grand scale. All the buildings there, down to the humblest garden shed (*above*), are designed to be eco-friendly.

Known locally as 'the wish cabin', this humble wooden building (*above*) stands on land above the sea, just north of San Francisco. People use it as a sanctuary for meditation, prayer or just plain sitting. Its spare interior is decorated with small tokens of thanks garnered from the nearby beach – votive offerings of shells, pebbles or sea-worn glass.

The arbour (*left*) designed by Eliel Saarinen for his garden at Hvittsträsk as a dining area reflects a view of domestic design in which everything is considered part of a total composition. In this case, the actual trelliswork structure and the furniture combine delightfully to create an integrated ensemble, while still remaining related to the garden around.

At the heart of traditional Balinese architecture is the pavilion form, known as a *bale*, which has evolved over centuries. It may be used in a domestic setting, where its relative openness permits the occupants to participate readily in the life of the central courtyard of the typical Balinese housing complex. A sharply pitched roof and overhanging eaves provide protection against sun and heavy rains alike. Pavilions are also used within temple complexes, where a crown on the roof may indicate shrine status (*right*).

The influence of the south-east Asian style of open pavilion architecture has been felt all around the Pacific rim. These two examples (*above left* and *right*) – Australian and Balinese respectively – show the form adapted to exactly the sort of casual seating arrangements which promote the leisurely enjoyment of an alfresco afternoon.

This poolside extension to a Los Angeles house (*above*) also looks to have been inspired by the principles of pavilion architecture. It permits the easy passage from inside to outside, and the natural-looking materials of its construction, especially those of the roof, seem entirely appropriate in the context of the planting beyond.

This poolside construction (*opposite*) strikes an audacious note in the midst of the Atacama desert, Chile, where a leisure group has developed a luxury hotel just outside the town of San Pedro. In contrast to the ruggedly dramatic landscape around, there is a well-defined and ordered look about this scene, perhaps an antidote to the rigours of the more adventurous pursuits available to guests. This self-conscious design could not be further from the intuitively placed table and chairs outside the door of this small farmhouse in Provence (*right*), which itself almost seems to be a part of the surrounding countryside.

CHAPTER 4

BRINGING THE OUTSIDE IN

Alfresco Decorations

The subtleties and ambiguities of alfresco living and design are the subject of the photographs in this chapter. Many of them are concerned with ways in which the outside can illuminate the interior – how, for instance, the peace and tranquility of gardens can be brought inside as an influence, without compromising the comforts of life indoors. Tables and chairs, originally intended for outside use, possibly weathered and showing the patina of age, open up new perspectives in interior decoration. Such articles of furniture may even reflect the natural world in their roughness of texture and the unfinished, untreated state of the materials from which they are made. Other examples of the decorative impact of the outside include designs which incorporate forms and motifs from the natural world and the use of the found objects of alfresco living as ornament: dried leaves and flowers, seed pods, pebbles, driftwood and herbs fresh from the garden.

Most of the houses and apartments illustrated achieve the effect of letting the outside in by the liberal use of glass as, effectively, a material for walls, thus diminishing the distinction between inside and outside. In some cases, rooms appear to relate seamlessly to the verandas, terraces or gardens surrounding them; others, notably those in the south-east Asian architectural style, achieve a similar effect by the use of wall-screens which can be removed to leave a house open to whatever is going on outside. Especially exciting are the designs where normally secluded rooms – bathrooms and bedrooms, for instance – open directly to an outside area.

In conclusion, this chapter ends with a mini photographic essay on an extraordinary Los Angeles house in which interior and exterior, living spaces and garden, seem almost indistinguishable from each other and whose very form seems part of an organic world.

Novel ways of bringing the outside in: flap windows perforated with Matisse-inspired motifs open up this Venice, California, apartment to the outside world (*above*).

The classic Balinese pavilion (*above*) permits the interior to be opened up to the outside. In this setting, the simplicity of the furniture and the flat-weave rug strikes exactly the right decorative note.

Earthenware pots and a spareness in the arrangement of furniture are the sophisticated high-points of a Balinese pavilion, open on three sides to the surrounding courtyards (*left above*).

Stones, bones, interestingly formed pieces of wood, seed pods and flowers: the objets trouvés of the alfresco world can make fascinating ornamental additions to any domestic environment, especially one that is already opened up to its natural surroundings. This engaging scene of clutter (*left below*), in which natural and man-made objects combine, is in the Kenyan home of an internationally renowned wildlife photographer, whose living space is permanently open to the surrounding vegetation.

Large expanses of glass open up the interior of this house to the views of the garden, towards which the whole interior furniture arrangement is directed (*right above*). And there is a special decorator's excitement in exposing those normally secluded rooms, such as bedrooms and bathrooms, to visual contact with the outside world (*right below*); this example is in a modern Irish house.

Natural, earthy materials, both in the form of the structure itself and as ornament and decoration, make this house at Zihuatenejo, on Mexico's Pacific coast, very much a part of the local landscape (*above*).

Balinese pavilion architecture on the grand scale (*above*): the size of this open-walled room and the majesty of the soaring roof/ceiling make the arrangements of elaborately carved furniture entirely in keeping with the whole scale of the design.

Even enclosed rooms can give off a strong sense of the freedom and relaxed manner of alfresco living, especially if they are flooded with light from an outside space. Both of these rooms in Marrakesh houses (*left* and *opposite*) receive plentiful daylight from neighbouring courtyards, almost certainly accompanied by the scent of fragrant plants and the sound of a gently bubbling water feature.

The subtle interplay of outside light and interior shade is fundamental to the charms of the traditional Moroccan house (*above*). This room, simple yet luxurious at the same time, is very much a space for looking out – to a garden or courtyard.

The overhanging eaves protect the traditional wooden Thai house (*above*), creating a veranda area as a transition between artificial structure and natural setting. During hot, humid periods, curtain walls can be opened up to allow air to circulate through the interior, while work, leisure and entertainment activities are conducted on the raised surface, shielded from the direct sunlight.

Using modern materials, this Balinese house (*left*), still manages to retain the sense of openness, of airiness, which is a characteristic of the traditional buildings of the island. Spaces flow into each other, while the expanses of glass ensure that the design is also inclusive of everything which lies around the house. Huge windows, too, flood the sitting-rooms of this Los Angeles modernist house with light (*opposite* and *overleaf*), reflecting the contemporary design vision of that city and its predilection for cool, logically managed environments. The whole house is permeated by outside light and even the arrangement of the furniture, including an overhanging Arco lamp, seems to have been made with the outside in mind rather than other focal points in the room. Open staircases emphasize the feeling of lightness and movement.

The ground floor of the same house (*preceding pages*) flows seamlessly out to terraces and gardens (*right*). Loft floors, again walled by glass, are cantilevered out over the main sitting area. And the fireplace, normally a major point of focus in more conventional interiors, has been reduced to a vestigial presence.

The formal interior of this house seems also to be reflected in the design of the garden, creating a balanced visual harmony between the two (*above*) while the wide arch of the glazing, provides a tent-like feeling to the room.

A room with a different kind of view: this stylish loft (*above*) looks out above the rooftops of Paris. The small narrow panels of glass seem to accentuate the panoramic proportions.

This hotel at Kiwayu, northern Kenya, is composed of twenty separate 'houses' (*above*). Each individual unit is built in the traditional manner of the region, using woven palm leaves to make the low roofs which shield the occupants from the glare of the sun yet permit the free circulation of air.

The open 'walls' of the typical Balinese house can be closed easily by blinds, or left open as they are for this attractive dining area (*above*).

Bringing the outside in as filtered light; this private residence on the Indonesian island of Sumbawa (*above*) is built entirely of local materials and in traditional style. Much of it is open to its surrounding garden, but can always be closed off by curtains or screens.

From the inside looking out: a casual seating arrangement by a window of a Paris apartment (*above*); the view is of a private garden, a welcome commodity in a built-up city.

In spite of its small scale, this town house in Nice (*left*) somehow manages to look spacious and airy, an effect of the lack of embellishment and the relatively extended window areas that give a permanent sense of the larger world outside.

Similarly, this house studio belonging to a Stockholm sculptor, (*opposite*) was planned to maximize the effect of bringing the outside in. Natural, found objects and copious foliage, combined with displays of the sculptor's own work, emphasize the exterior/interior relationship.

Quality of light and the immediate view can often combine to bring certain rooms under the immediate influence of the outside. For instance, this bathroom of a Los Angeles house (*above*) looks out through wrap-around windows directly on to the garden.

In another Los Angeles bathroom (*above*), glass doors and glossy surfaces ensure that the effects of luminosity from the large windows are extended even further.

A modern version of a Balinese pavilion (*above*) incorporates glass screen-walls to maintain the pervasive presence of the adjacent garden and courtyard all year round.

This cool, minimalist kitchen in a London house (*above*) immediately reflects all the available light flooding in through the arch from the patio garden; the end wall is made wholly of glass.

The disappearing wall: glass replaces masonry in this Paris apartment (*above*) to give the occupants a welcome sight of the well-planted terrace. By placing the furniture and pots very close to the glass, the barrier between inside and outside seems to disappear.

In yet another Paris duplex (*above*), extra large windows, faced by a display of rustic Provençal pots, give on to the terrace.

The furniture in a Mexico City hotel room (*above*) is deliberately directed towards the glass wall and terrace.

A secluded terrace serves as a visual extension of a modernist interpretation of a traditional Japanese bathroom (*above*).

The essence of the alfresco lifestyle is in the continuity of life outside with life inside. This is nowhere better expressed than in the domestic architecture where the more intimate rooms of a dwelling can open out immediately to a terrace, veranda, or even a garden. Here, this stylish bathroom in a house in the Queensland rain-forest gives directly on to a terrace that in turn overlooks the trees (*left*).

An uncluttered, minimalist bedroom gives directly on to a roof-terrace in this conversion of a traditional London Victorian house (*right*). Privacy is ensured by retaining high sections of the original walls, while a feeling of continuity is sustained by having the decking reflect the dimensions and direction of the indoor flooring.

Colours, textures, forms and light combine to create in these two rooms a complex relationship to the outside. Light floods into a New York apartment (*opposite*) to illuminate a setting with peculiar resonances of the natural world in the central table display and the curvilinear forms of the rustic chairs. In a Paris apartment, too, the furniture almost looks as though it could have been reclaimed from some setting beyond the light-filled windows (*above*).

Furniture and free-standing ornament in this Paris apartment (*above*) are all strangely suggestive of terrace and garden life.

A painter of flowers has transformed this former boiler-maker's warehouse in Montreuil, east of Paris, into a showcase for her work (*above*). 'Adirondack-style' chairs complete the feeling of agreeable rusticity.

Climbing plants have turned this conservatory of a house on the Île de Ré (*above*) into a marvellously leafy adjunct to a kitchen.

Keeping natural appearances: the frame of this four-poster bed in an Australian house has preserved the original forms of the untreated wood (*left*), turning the piece into an ironic rustic metaphor.

These articles of furniture (*right*) were made by an artist who works entirely in local woods on the Indonesian island of Sumbawa. In this, he has taken up the traditions of the local community, many of whom produce artefacts, including boats, carved from solid wood.

Overleaf
A room in the Adirondack Museum recreates a traditional rustic interior; the furniture, which almost looks as though it had been made for outside use, has all the roughness of birch bark and untreated wood.

The walls of this Provençal house (*above*) are covered with boldly painted wall-hangings depicting natural forms; the outside has thus been stylized and brought inside.

Simple cane furniture and decorative vegetation in a Corsican house (*above*) refer gently and subtly back to lives conducted largely outside in a benevolent climate. The austerity of the room is relieved by the bunch of dill, brought fresh from the garden.

Nothing enlivens an interior as much as fresh flowers, especially if they have been drawn directly from the countryside. And in this house at Uzès, Provence, the garden seems only too close beyond the window embrasure (*left*). An ornate blue-and-white Chinese vase filled with an armful of broom becomes a dramatic centrepiece in the midst of the sturdy country furniture of a Tuscan farmhouse (*opposite*).

Natural materials in formal arrangements: the summer solstice festival in Sweden is celebrated by the making of wreaths and hanging bunches of corn and wild flowers (*left* and *opposite*).

Photographs and other man-made artefacts mingle with the found objects of the natural world – bones, stones, wood – to create an engaging display of clutter which effectively unites the world of artifice with the natural surroundings of this relaxed Kenyan dwelling (*left*).

The use of natural objects to create formal displays, designs and patterns is yet another important aspect of introducing the outside to the inside (*right*). This Belgian interior is embellished with unusual organic forms, including dried pods and leaf-form stencils. The orderly appearance of the arrangements makes them all the more striking: organic matter as carefully disposed ornament. More informal but similarly intriguing is this display of dried seed-pods in the Goan home of a botanist (*overleaf*).

LARGE-LEAVED

Reflections of a natural world in the form of found objects used for interior or courtyard ornament: twigs, leaves, fragments of classical architecture engraved with plant forms evoke an outside world within. Carefully bound bundles of twigs surround the blind fireplace of a Paris apartment (*left*). In Hammamet, Tunisia, the owners of an elegant villa have hit upon an especially stylish mode of decoration for their courtyard: collected fragments of classical statuary and stone carving painstakingly arranged in seemingly random fashion (*opposite*).

SAR F IMP CA
MI TRIB POT
II FRATRI DI
RAIAN
D
D

Plant forms have always been a major source of inspiration for designers and architects in many different cultures. Their effect is especially meaningful when they are used in places – doors, windows, paving – where outside meets inside: floral tiles in Bangkok (*far left above*); a carved arch in Oaxaca, Mexico (*left above*); etched glass in Barcelona (*far left below*); an Art Deco floral motif in Shanghai (*left below*); leaf-patterned paving tiles in Bali (*opposite*); bird and leaf ceiling decoration in a Roman palace (*overleaf*).

The house illustrated on this and the following pages could be legitimately described as the ultimate alfresco dwelling. Even the irregular forms of the masonry somehow seem to imitate natural growth. In the outside kitchen area (*left*), for instance, shelves and sink look almost organic amid the planting of the cactus garden; even the faucets are concealed within a natural-looking masonry block.

Planting is used sculpturally and architecturally in relation to the solid structures of the complex. For instance, a 'wall' of cactus acts as a screen for a low-level sitting room, just by the exterior kitchen area (*right above*). Its effectiveness and the sheer drama it adds to the interior can be judged from this view from within the room itself (*right below*). A mosaic design set into the floor like an architectural fragment reinforces the impression that interior and exterior are continuations of each other.

The pathways around the same house (*preceding pages*) meander in a natural, organic way – an effect heightened by the use of irregular pebbles to define their course around the planting (*above*).

Patches of planting occur at intervals around the complex, breaking down strict definitions of house and garden (*above*).

The cacti are varied but, combined with pebbles and boulders, they always create dramatic impact by their stark forms (*above*).

A water feature, just beside the kitchen/ dining room (*above* and *overleaf*) is crossed by slabs of rock which serve as stepping stones.

The water feature leads directly to the wide entrance arch of the kitchen/ dining room (*opposite* and *above*). A rustic simplicity characterizes both furniture and fixtures in this part of the house (*overleaf*). A classic beamed ceiling covers the dining area which is defined at floor level by a rug-like mosaic in earth colours. The work-surfaces of the kitchen incorporate old worked stone and natural rock.

In the evening and at night, candlelight and underwater lighting confer a warm glow on the areas around the water feature (*above*). Embellishments here include a number which enhance the overall feeling of naturalness: large earthenware pots and a monumental upturned oil jar (*above* and *opposite*).

The main sitting room of the house (*right*) is dominated by a huge fireplace in rough-hewn stone and fronted by natural rocks. In front of the fireplace a low-level seating and conversation area has been created by simply strewing a number of Oriental rugs on the floor and the addition of four traditional nomadic saddle chairs.

Just as around the outside of the house, there are no visible concessions to modern technology. Candlelight subtly changes the appearance of the central sitting area and its sculptural open staircase (*above* and *opposite*).

CHAPTER 5

LIVING OUTSIDE

The Alfresco Lifestyle

Effectively a celebration of outside living, the images of this chapter open up the definition of 'alfresco' to include a wider world of open-air markets, restaurants and even those focal points of street life, the food vendors. This is a world away from the house-related confines of verandas, terraces and gardens, yet the true spirit of alfresco is abundantly present – the will to enjoy to the full the wide 'outside'. Perhaps nothing reflects this spirit so completely as the images of the picnic, where the simple laying down of a cloth and the presence of a well-filled basket or hamper creates a convivial focus for any group.

Here, too, are some classic examples of the alfresco lifestyle, drawn mainly from the Mediterranean area. Delightful table settings in gardens shaded from the sun herald the pleasures of local produce, country wines and post-prandial conversation. More often than not, such arrangements have an engagingly casual air about them, typified perhaps by an impromptu barbecue, but sometimes a pergola or awning does provide a finishing touch.

And finally to images of realization of the alfresco goal: the facility to carry out all those activities associated with the interior in an exterior setting. In this case, showers and tubs act as metaphors for the ultimate in alfresco lifestyle. It is fitting and appropriate, too, that several of these final images reflect life on the island of Bali, whose people, climate and culture, especially manifested in its architecture, have made the complex relationship between interior and exterior a whole way of life.

Enjoyment of the alfresco lifestyle does not necessarily demand an elaborately constructed patio, courtyard, terrace or veranda. Sometimes it is simply a matter of spreading out a cloth with lunch to create a centre of enjoyment, even in such unlikely places as the arid Atacama desert, Chile (*left above*). And in Hama, groups of Syrians meet beneath arcades to enjoy a convivial repast (*left below*).

By the water's edge on the shores of the island of Porquerolles, southern France, a family sets out to enjoy the contents of a well-stocked picnic basket (*right*).

The delights of alfresco living and eating can of course take many forms other than the private, secluded and intimate. This wedding feast in a Romanian village (*above*) is clearly an occasion for celebrating local traditions and community living outside.

This restaurant in Manila (*above*) adds another dimension to the pleasures of alfresco dining: the feet of the diners are refreshed by a brook flowing beneath the tables.

Overleaf
In a broader context, the meaning of alfresco can be extended to include all the social experiences of outside living, especially those associated with food and its preparation and with the joy of communal activity. Streetlife in general and markets in particular generate areas of outside focus for any community, offering opportunities for the exchange of views as well as money and produce. Here, dusk falls over the magnificent main market in Marrakesh.

The vendor, common to so many cultures (*these pages*), provides a point of contact at street level for the communities of many cities.

Overleaf
Simple things done well: a permanent rustic table in a dappled grove of a Provence garden provides the surface for the preliminary stages of an alfresco meal (*pp. 226–227*). Again in Provence (*pp. 228–229*), a simple meal of local produce under pine trees takes shape with the aid of a makeshift barbecue: veal, beef, shallots, marrow bones – somehow food does taste better outside!

Traditional garden furniture strikes the only humble chord in this elaborate table setting on the terrace of a house on the island of Porquerolles, southern France (*above*).

On a cliff-top near Monte Carlo, this terrace-cum-pergola provides the owners of the house with a year-round dining area and views over the sea (*above*).

Undoubtedly the countries of the Mediterranean enjoy many of the essentials of alfresco living – plentiful sun, good food and a generally relaxed lifestyle. It would be hard to imagine anything more alluring than these two permanently sited and ingenious terrace eating areas – the one in Carpentras, Provence (*left*), the other attached to a Moroccan house (*opposite*).

More Mediterranean – and more examples showing that the enjoyment of life around the house and the pleasures of eating alfresco need not depend on specially constructed courtyards or terraces. Here, in Provence (*left above*), and on the Île de Ré (*left below*), it has been sufficient to set up table and chairs in an agreeable spot – the meal and conversation take care of the rest.

Certainly, in the majority of alfresco eating spots illustrated on these pages, the presence of planting and foliage has been very important, either in the form of surrounding trees and shrubs, as in this French garden (*right above*), or more formally arranged over trellis or pergola, as in this Sicilian garden (*right below*). Trained climbers and potted plants on the terrace behind this house in Carpentras (*overleaf*) complete an almost impossibly idyllic scene.

Alfresco, however, can embrace many different settings and experiences, sometimes very different from leafy Mediterranean terraces. In the Atacama desert, Chile, a hotel complex has found imaginative ways of reaching out to its arid surroundings: by building pathways and bathing platforms for the use of guests away from the main buildings (*left*). A terrace of a modernist Belgian house remains a place for quiet contemplation all the year round (*opposite*). And back to the Mediterranean in Saint-Rémy-de-Provence (*overleaf*) to demonstrate alfresco informality: the table and chairs have surely just been brought outside from the kitchen to create the simplest, most relaxed dining area.

Many and varied are the kinds of furniture which can be successfully pressed into service for alfresco living. This shaded swing seat – here in a garden in Phuket, Thailand – is curiously suggestive of the nineteen-twenties and cocktails (*left*)!

This day-bed is entirely of the outside in that it is made of driftwood gathered from a beach in Corsica (*right*) to create what is effectively furniture-sculpture. The rest of the house is also furnished with similar creations.

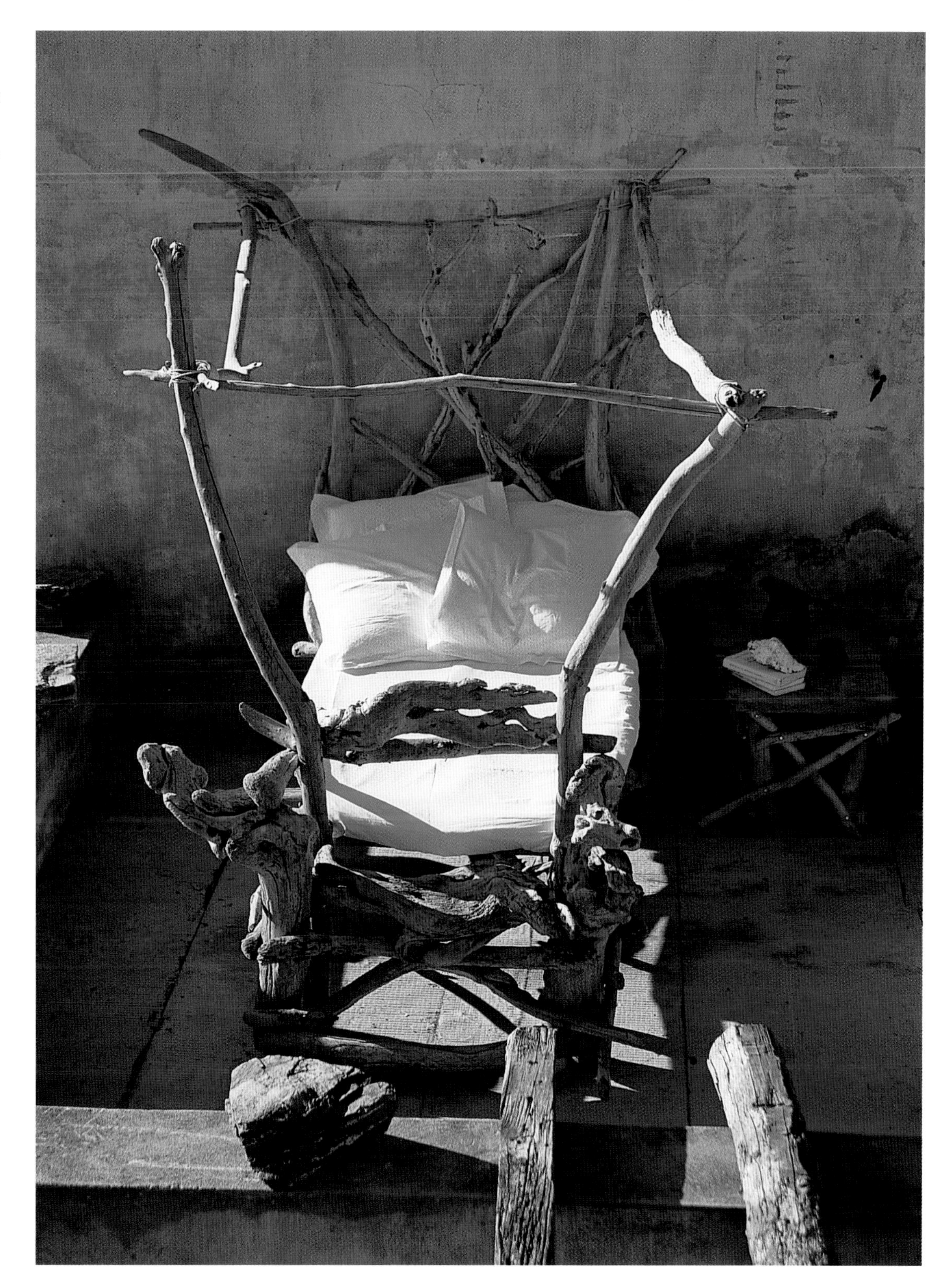

The ultimate goal of alfresco living must surely be the facility to carry out all the activities associated with life within the home in contexts which involve contact with the outside: cooking, eating, sleeping, bathing all seem strangely more exciting in the open air. But the creation of suitable environments to enjoy an alfresco lifestyle demands design sensitivity to immediate surroundings to achieve that satisfying feeling of rightness. All of these shower installations, for instance, embody exactly that feeling in their design and setting – from Mexico (*far left above* and *opposite*), to Bali (*left above* and *far left below*), to Marrakesh (*left below*) – mainly because of the intelligent use of local materials and design practices – simple solutions in environments rich in natural features.

From Morocco (*above left*) to Mexico (*above right*) the outside tub brings an ultimate refinement to alfresco bathing and living.

Two hot tubs in Balinese gardens (*above left* and *right*) evoke that island's style of living in which interior and exterior can often seem interchangable.

As a final note to this celebration of alfresco, what could be more fitting than these images of outside living on Bali, so expressive of the subtleties of relating inside and outside (*left* and *opposite*)?

Page numbers in *italic* refer to illustrations

Q

R

S

T

ACKNOWLEDGMENTS

Designed by Stafford Cliff
Index compiled by Anna Bennett

First published in the United Kingdom in 2005 by
Thames & Hudson Ltd
181A High Holborn
London WC1V 7QX

www.thamesandhudson.com

British Library Cataloguing-in-Publication Data
A catalogue record for this book is available from the British Library

ISBN 13: 978-0-500-51222-7
ISBN 10: 0-500-51222-1

Printed and bound in Singapore
by CS Graphics

The photographs in this book are the result of many years of travelling around the world to carry out commissions for various magazines and clients. Very special thanks is due therefore to all the many people who have helped to make the realization of this project possible, including Martine Albertin, Béatrice Amagat, Catherine Ardouin, Françoise Ayxandri, Marion Bayle, Jean-Pascal Billaud, Anna Bini, Marie-Claire Blanckaert, Barbara Bourgois, Marie-France Boyer, Marianne Chedid, Alexandra D'Arnoux, Catherine de Chabaneix, Jean Demachy, Emmanuel de Toma, Geneviève Dortignac, Jérôme Dumoulin, Marie-Claude Dumoulin, Lydia Fiasoli, Jean-Noel Forestier, Marie Kalt, Françoise Labro, Anne Lefèvre, Hélène Lafforgue, Catherine Laroche, Nathalie Leffol, Blandine Leroy, Marianne Lohse, Chris O'Byrne, Christine Puech, José Postic, Nello Renault, Daniel Rozensztroch, Elisabeth Selse, Suzanne Slesin, Caroline Tiné, Francine Vormèse, Claude Vuillermet, Suzanne Walker, Rosaria Zucconi and Martin Bouazis.

Our thanks also goes to those who allowed us to photograph their houses and apartments: Adirondack Museum, Jean-Marie Amat, Mea Argentieri, Avril, Claire Basler, Peter Beard, Bébèche, Luisa Becaria, Dominique Bernard, Dorothée Boissier, Carole Bracq, Susie and Mark Buell, Michel Camus, Laurence Clark, Anita Coppet and Jean-Jacques Driewir, David Cornell, Bertile Cornet, Jane Cumberbatch, Geneviève Cuvelier, Ricardo Dalasi, Anne and Pierre Damour, Joan K. Davidson, Catherine Dénoual, Dominique and Pierre Bénard Dépalle, Phillip Dixon, Ann Dong, Patrice Doppelt, Philippe Duboy, Christian Duc, Jan Duclos Maïm, Bernard Dufour, Explora Group, Flemish Primitives, Florian (Venice), Michèle Fouks, Pierre Fuger, Massimiliano Fuksas, Teresa Fung and Teresa Roviras, Henriette Gaillard, His Majesty the Maharajah Gaj Sing Ji, Jean and Isabelle Garçon, John MacGlenaghan, Fiora Gondolfi, Annick Goutal and Alain Meunier, Murielle Grateau, Michel and Christine Guérard, Yves and Michèle Halard, Hotel Le Sénéchal, Hotel Samod Haveli, Anthony Hudson, Ann Huybens, Patrick T'Hoft, Igor and Lili, Michèle Iodice, Paul Jacquette, Hellson, Jolie Kelter and Michael Malcé, Amr Khalil, Dominique Kieffer, Kiwayu Safari Village, Lawrence and William Kriegel, Philippe Labro, Karl Lagerfeld, François Lafanour, Nad Laroche, Rudolph Thomas Leimbacher, Philippe Lévèque and Claude Terrijn, Marion Lesage, Lizard Island Hotel, Luna, Catherine Margaretis, Marongiu, Mathias, Valérie Mazerat and Bernard Ghèzy, Jean-Louis Mennesson, Ilaria Miani, Mies van der Rohe Pavilion (Barcelona), Anna Moï, Leonardo Mondadori, Jacqueline Morabito, Christine Moussière, Paola Navone, Christine Nicaise, Christian Neirynck, Jean Oddes, Catherine Painvin, John Pawson, Christiane Perrochon, Phong Pfeufer, Françoise Pialoux les Terrasses, Alberto Pinto, Stéphane Plassier, Morgan Puett, Bob Ramirez, Riad Dar Amane, Riad Dar Kawa, Yagura Rié, Guillaume Saalburg, Holly Salomon, Jérôme-Abel Séguin, Jocelyne and Jean-Louis Sibuet, Siegrid and her cousins, Valérie Solvi, Tapropane Villa, Patis and Tito Tesoro, Richard Texier, Jérôme Tisné, Doug Tomkins, Anna and Patrice Touron, Christian Tortu, Armand Ventilo, Véronique Vial, Barbara de Vries, Thomas Wegner, Quentin Wilbaux, Catherine Willis.

Thanks is also due to the following magazines for allowing us to include photographs originally published by them: *Architectural Digest* (French Edition), *Atmosphère, Coté Sud, Elle, Elle à Table, Elle Décoration, Elle Décor Italie, Madame Figaro, Maison Française, Marie Claire, Marie Claire Idées, Marie Claire Maison, The World of Interiors.*

The illustration on pp. 228–229 is reproduced from *Under the Sun – French Country Cooking* by kind permission of the author Caroline Conran and the publisher, Pavilion Books Ltd.